BRAHMINS INDIA CASTE SYSTEM

EVERYTHING YOU NEED TO KNOW ABOUT THE HISTORY AND ORIGIN OF BRAHMINS,BHUMIHARS,KSHATRIYAS,VAISHYA AND SUDRAS CASTE SYSTEM IN INDIA

VEENA SAMRA

Made with ❤ on the Notion Press Platform
www.notionpress.com

Contents

Title Page

BRAHMINS INDIA CASTE SYSTEM

Everything you Need to Know about The History and Origin of Brahmins,Bhumihars,Kshatriyas,Vaishya and Sudras Caste System in India

Veena Samra

CHAPTER ONE

INTRODUCTION

Having persisted for about the last three thousand years, India's caste system is widely regarded as the prototypical caste system and the longest surviving example of social stratification on the planet. According to their profession, Hindus are divided into one of four varnas (classes) under India's caste system.

A Brahmin is a personification of wisdom since he or she belongs to the highest caste (varna) in Hinduism.

The Kshatriyas, who are the second-highest of the four varnas and are traditionally thought of as warriors and nobles, are the most noble of the four castes.

The Vaishyas are the third caste, and they are businesspeople.

The Sudras (workers) are the lowest caste in the Hindu social hierarchy.

CHAPTER TWO

The Indian caste system

There are four varnas under India's caste system.

Just what is the Indian Caste System?

The caste system is a social stratification system based on birth order. About the year 1500 B.C., a group of people called the Aryans migrated to India and established a caste system. The Indian caste system is made up of two distinct ideas: varna and jati, and it has evolved throughout the course of Indian history as a mechanism of social control, notably during the Mughal Empire and the British Raj.

Varna

The term varna originates from Sanskrit and means "caste" or "society" in English. The Vedas are the source of the Varna social stratification (the oldest texts of Hinduism). In Vedic culture, the caste system was known as varna (c. 1100 – c. 500 BCE). The varna system was created to equalize workloads among citizens. According to the Varna system, there are four distinct social strata:

Brahmins, religious leaders and academics

Kshatriyas are traditionally considered to be both warriors and aristocrats.

Farmers, merchants, and traders are all considered Vaishyas.

Laborers; Shudras

If all four varnas do well at what they're supposed to do, then society as a whole is thriving and robust and its members may exercise their freedom without fear of oppression.

Jati

The Sanskrit word jati means "birth" from the root jaha. A jati is any society where intermarriage is obligatory due to shared ancestry (marriage within the same group).

Each jati had its own set of rites and traditions for preserving the integrity of the varnas and establishing permanent order. A person's jati regulated who they could and could not eat and drink with, socialize with, and marry, as well as their employment and social standing in society.

Each of the four varnas has several subgroups, known as jatis. Each of the over 3,000 distinct jatis may be categorized as belonging to one of the four varnas.

CHAPTER THREE

Origins of the Caste System

It is widely held, in accordance with Hindu religious theory and scripture, that these four divisions all descended from Brahma, the Hindu deity of creation. The Rig Veda claims that the first man, Purush, utilized his body to give rise to the several castes that make up human civilization. The Brahmins sprang from Purush's brain, the Kshatriyas from his limbs, the Vaishyas from his torso, and the Shudras from his feet.

A group known as Dalits (or "Untouchables")

Dalits, often known as "untouchables," were excluded from the caste system because they lacked a jati designation. The Untouchables were a group of people who worked outside of the caste system and were assigned tasks that required them to come into contact with body fluids, such as cleaning toilets and collecting rubbish. These jobs were seen as the lowest of the low and were not eligible for a jati because of it.

The Brahmins are India's highest caste.

According to Hindu literature, Brahmins are at the pinnacle of the varna system because they are descended from Purush, the Supreme Being. Among the Brahmin are ministers and educators. They have the highest education possible, have the right to interpret religious texts and offer sacrifices to gods, and are able to interpret religious texts and offer sacrifices to gods. They were responsible for imparting knowledge of cultural practices, interpreting religious discourse, and reporting on agricultural harvests. They also played pivotal roles in academia, industry, and politics.

Despite their social status, Brahmins are prohibited from engaging in some occupations and practices, such as those involving the production or sale of weapons or poisons, the slaughter of animals, the capture of wildlife, and the hunting of humans. The Brahmin community is known for its severe austerity and voluntary poverty. They follow many of the other tenets of Hinduism as strictly as they do their adherence to a vegetarian diet.

Chastity is highly valued among Brahmin women, and most exclusively marry within the caste. Inter-caste marriages are frowned upon since they are thought to result in the birth of dishonorable children. Nonetheless, Kshatriya and Vaishya are permitted to wed a Brahmin under certain circumstances. Men of the Shudra caste are not permitted.

Almost 5% of India's population identifies as Brahmin. Some live in southern Indian states like Tamil Nadu, Karnataka, and Kerala, but they are in the minority compared to their prevalence in northern Indian states like Uttar Pradesh and Andhra Pradesh.

Kshatriyas are the second highest of the four castes, or Varnas.

According to Hindu mythology, Kshatriyas were born in Purush's arms and hence occupy the position of the highest caste in the varna system.

Kshatriyas are those who govern over others and wield temporal power. They're in command of the military and get to rake in a ton of money via tax collections. They serve as the Brahmin elite's personal bodyguards.

Kshatriyas are socially expected to begin their training as leaders at a young age, studying weapons, battle, penance, austerity, administration, moral behavior, and justice.

Because of their riches and status, the Kshatriya caste was allowed to indulge in things like drinking beer and eating meat. Differentiating them from the Brahmins are these features.

Although Kshatriyas are not restricted from marrying women of other varnas, they are more likely to find happiness with another Kshatriya or a Brahmin lady. The majority of India's Kshatriyas may be found in the country's northern regions.

Vaishya is the third-highest Varna.

The Vaishyas are the third highest varna, written as deriving from the first man's thighs, and are considered to be the ordinary people.

There is a preponderance of Vaishyas in business and agricultural fields. They lack governmental power but prosper economically due to their proximity to trade; hence, many of them choose the professions of traders, merchants, landowners, and moneylenders.

Vaishyas provide for Kshatriyas and Brahmins via sacrifice, gifts, agriculture, and taxation. While Vaishyas perform a crucial role in society by providing craftsmen with access to technical education, they remain a social outcast.

The Sudras are India's lowest caste.

According to Hindu belief, Sudras are the lowest of the four castes since they are descended directly from Purush's foot. Craftspeople, manual workers, and high-ranking servants and artisans make up the bulk of this group; this includes the food preparers and servers.

About half of India's people are Sudras, making them the most numerous caste. Many members of this caste, which is the default varna, are the offspring of upper-caste members or even of Untouchables and Sudras.

Sudras are considered to be the lowest caste in Hinduism and are therefore denied many of the privileges enjoyed by those of higher castes, such as "twice-birth" (initiation into a Vedic school) and the ability to offer certain sacrifices, due to the widespread belief that they are the product of the ground.

To what extent did the caste system really function?

During its many centuries of existence, the caste system in India has played a crucial part in determining not just how individuals are employed but also how they feel about themselves and the world.

The interactions between persons in various social strata, notably, have been governed by it. Separation, hierarchy, and inherited specialization are all results.

One's Profession Is Determined by One's Caste

The Rig Veda states that all four varnas are derived from the same body that Brahma used to create humanity.

In Hinduism, the soul (the head) is sacred beyond compare, whereas the body (the rest of the person) is not. Therefore, the Brahmins (originating from the neck) are in charge of spiritual and intellectual matters, the Kshatriyas (originating from the upper body) handle political and military matters, the Vaishyas (originating from the lower body) serve as the upper castes' support staff, and the

Sudras (originating from the feet) are the working class.

CHAPTER FOUR

Hereditary Caste System

Your caste is determined by that of your parents, and your children will inherit your caste if you have any. A person's varna is decided at birth. Similarly, his or her jita (occupation group) is predetermined and cannot be modified throughout the course of a person's lifetime.

The admission to a Vedic school or official social acceptance are two examples of rites of passage that have allowed some people to alter their caste. A few people choose to marry outside of their caste.

Caste determines one's way of life and the relationships one may have.

Many social groups adhere to different norms and standards based on their caste. If it is broken, the violator will face severe repercussions in the cosmos and the wrath of the faithful.

Contact between members of different castes was often frowned upon. Those in higher castes tended to congregate in urban areas, while those in lower castes tended to scatter over the countryside. Brahmins did not eat or drink from Shudras or vice versa, water wells were not shared, etc. The social standing of meat eaters was lower than that of vegetarians and abstainers.

Hindus could (typically) only marry within their caste to prevent members of lower castes from crossing the caste barrier via marriage. Untouchables may include couples who marry across social classes.

In order to improve your low caste in the "next life," you must adhere firmly to Brahmin teaching, keep oneself holy, and assist the Brahmin nobility (reincarnation).

CHAPTER FIVE

Today's Indian Caste Structure

In modern times, India passed a legislation officially doing away with the caste system. Identity documents issued in India do not include a caste designation. A lot of the constraints of India's caste system were lifted once the country gained its freedom. Nowadays, tensions between different castes are lower. The practice of intercaste marriage is on the rise, and so is the practice of sharing meals across social groups.

In India, both the Sudra and the untouchables have access to formal schooling. More and more individuals are marrying outside of their caste, altering the fate of their ancestors just as many have become physicians, attorneys, and professors. Several people from lower social classes have left their homelands to find success elsewhere. Two Indian presidents, Narayanan (in 1997) and Ram Nath Kovind (in 2017), were once considered "untouchables."

The Indian government instituted a number of positive discrimination laws, including quotas for members of lower castes in government, work, and education, to aid the downtrodden people of low castes and untouchables. Communities and castes were categorized by the thousands by local administrations so that these rules could be implemented. Scheduled Castes (SC) and Scheduled Tribes (ST) were created for the lowest social strata, while Other Backward Classes were created for the next rung up the social ladder but remained at the bottom economically (OBC).

Notwithstanding contemporary India's affirmative discrimination policy, the lower caste groups have not risen beyond their original socioeconomic standing. And affluent neighborhoods maintain their status atop the social order. Dalits continue to perform the lowest-paying occupations in India, while Brahmins maintain their status at the top of the caste system as the country's elite professionals.

Casteism and the Indian social hierarchy structure have both persisted for almost three thousand years, making rapid transformation unlikely. The caste system in India has a long way to go before it is eradicated.

CHAPTER SIX

ORIGIN OF THE INDIAN CASTE SYSTEM

Origins of the Caste System

Maybe you were introduced to the concept of caste while studying global history. Maybe you saw it as an obsolete method from the distant past. Yet this social divide, unlike others we've seen throughout history, continues to shape daily life in India. You're limited in everything from the kind of work you can have to the type of water you can drink. So let me back up a little. Because of Hinduism's emphasis on karma and rebirth, the caste system has persisted for centuries.

The Hindu caste system, which has been in place for over three thousand years, classifies people into Brahmins, Kshatriyas, Vaishyas, and Shudras according to their former lives, their karma, and their family tree. Many Hindus attribute the origin of the caste system to Brahma, the Hindu God of creation, with the Brahmins standing in for Brahma's eyes and mind and thus typically filling the roles of teachers and priests, the Kshatriyas for his arms and performing the roles of soldiers and business owners, the Vaishyas for his legs and carrying out the roles of farmers and merchants, and the Shudras for their feet and filling the roles of manual laborers.

The four major social groups are as follows:

Brahmins are considered to be the most prestigious and elite caste in Indian society. The roles of priest and teacher are common vocations for these persons.

Kshatriyas are the members of the middle caste. Traditional societies have a tendency to label these individuals as "warriors." Farmers, traders, and shopkeepers make up a large portion of their workforce.

The Waishyas are the third caste in Hindu society. Farmers, traders, and shopkeepers make up a large portion of this group.

The fourth caste, known as Shudras. They are often the ones that do physical work.

Even though there are four primary castes, the system further divides the people of India into thousands of sub-castes. Another group, known as the Untouchables or Dalits, exists who are so reviled by society that they are not included in any caste. They are utterly rejected by regular people. not allowed to associate with people of higher social status.

Some Information About India's Caste System

The Hindu god Brahma is a quadruped with four arms and a phallus. Brahma's descending manifestation of the four basic classes described above is the basis of the caste system.

Mahatma Gandhi devoted a significant portion of his life to achieving racial parity for the Dalits (Untouchables). Untouchables were first referred to by his term, "Harijan," which means "children of God."

Your birthcaste is determined by your family's caste.

The Laws of Manu, a sacred Hindu scripture written approximately 250 B.C., contains the first known description of the caste system.

Dalits are so stigmatized for their perceived impurity that they are not allowed to drink from the same water fountains, walk along the same streets, or eat at the same restaurants as those of better social status.

While many major Indian cities have moved away from caste's overwhelming impact, the system is still quite widespread in rural areas, with caste being a major factor in defining where one may live, what one can do for a living, who one can talk to, and even what one's basic rights are.

This system is so ingrained in the national psyche that its norms and after-effects will last for generations.

It was the fall of the Mughal Empire and the British colonial rule in India that ultimately led to the development of the Caste System as we know it today. The Persianate Mughal dynasty, which descended from the Chagatai Turco-Mongols, dominated most of the Indian subcontinent. Because of the passing of this age, there was a swell in the number of those who saw themselves as strong and allied themselves with monarchs and clergy. In 1860 and again in 1920, the British colonial authority furthered this trend by dividing Indians along caste lines. They restricted access to high-status occupations to those from the highest social classes. In 1920, the colonial administration instituted a program that set aside a portion of government positions for members of the lower castes. With India's independence from the British Empire in 1947, new policies were implemented that benefited the country's lower caste inhabitants. The Supreme Court of India took a number of progressive steps toward racial equality in the year 1950. of the Indian constitution makes it unlawful to discriminate against members of the lower castes.

Brahmins:

Brahmin means "Ultimate Self" or "the first of the gods" in Sanskrit. In Vedic Hinduism, Brahmin is the highest of the Varnas. It is estimated in "The Joshua project" that 60,481,000 persons in India belong to the Brahmin caste. Around 4.3% of India's overall population. Priests belong to the Brahmin Varna, and within this caste there are smaller groups known as gotras. These sub-castes are made up of Brahmins, however there are many more that exist due to the wide variety of Brahmin traditions. Not all of its members are priests; some have worked as teachers, legislators, researchers, physicians, journalists, poets, farmers, or politicians. According to Nancy Auerbach's book Living Hinduism, the Brahmin are linked to Sanatana Dharma, which is a code of ethics or a way of life in early Hinduism in order to reach "mosksha," a feeling of emancipation and enlightenment. The Brahmins, a powerful Varna in India, discriminated against members of other castes as the caste system evolved.

The majority of India's Brahmin population lives in the northern states of Uttar Pradesh and Andhra Pradesh, with smaller numbers also living in the southern states of Tamil Nadu, Karnataka, and Kerala. The Brahmin split into the northern Panch Gour and southern Panch Dravida because of this geographical separation (Southerners). The central Vindhya mountain range in India separates these two communities nearly exactly in half.

The word Brahmin derives from the Hindu concept of Brahman, a divine energy. The first properly educated priest to perform a sacrifice was given the term Brahmin.

When the Vedic era drew to a close about 1000 B.C., the word "Brahmin" started to be used interchangeably with "priest" to refer to all members of the priestly caste. In 900 B.C., the Brahmins began to form exogamous clans that controlled ritual and limited marriage freedom. Marriage between members of different castes is still seen as socially unacceptable in many parts of the world. The mythical beginnings of the Brahmin may be found in the Rig Veda, one of the holiest Hindu scriptures. A member of the Hindu trinity, Prajapati (King of Beings) is considered synonymous with Brahma (Creator) and was himself sacrificed by his offspring. According to legend, it was this sacrifice that birthed the cosmos, and the Brahmin was born from his lips.

There is a common misconception that all Brahmin are priests; in reality, however, they work in a broad range of fields. Some work in white-collar professions, although the majority of members are farmers. While Brahmins are not restricted in their career choices, only those born into the caste are permitted to enter the priesthood. The majority of people in this Community adhere to a vegetarian diet. As a social and spiritual duty, it is expected that Brahmins be fed during rituals. The male members of the Brahmin caste have more autonomy than their female counterparts. Although smoking and drinking are socially acceptable for males, they are taboo for women. There is also a difference in the minimum age that society considers a person "socially mature" enough to be married. Women may legally be married as early as the age of 18, whereas males often wait until they're much older. Parents often arrange marriages and promote monogamy. While widows are barred from remarrying, widowers are not. Women of the Brahmin caste in Indian culture may be ranked behind males in terms of power and prestige, yet they excel academically compared to other women in India.

In Hindu culture, Brahmins are often regarded as the most intelligent and powerful members of society. They are the ones who determine what is right and wrong for the rest of us to follow because of their position of authority. While Brahmins make up the vast majority of Hindu priests, other castes do have "holy experts," however their rank is not on par with that of a Brahmin.

Kshatriyas:

Kshatriya is derived from the Sanskrit word kshatra, which meaning "ruler." These privileges and perks are not earned by excellent leadership but rather through the possession of sovereign territory. Kshatriyas are the second highest social caste (Varna) in India. Twenty percent of the Indian population belongs to the higher castes, which are comprised of the Brahmin and the Kshatriya. The Kshatriya are the top of society, the rulers and warriors. As a civilization, they exist to serve as soldiers in times of conflict and as rulers during times of peace. They were responsible for keeping the populace safe, making sure everyone did their part, and helping each Individual progress spiritually. Furthermore, they are accountable for safeguarding the political cosmic order (dharma). Kshatriyas were originally elevated to their position because of their inherent talents, actions, and character (swabhava). Later on in the evolution of the caste system, merit stopped being a factor and rank became inherited instead.

It is stated that a "negative energy" emanated from Brahma as he was having children. The bad force materialized as Rakshasas, commonly known as demons, and they began to torment Brahma. In the end, Brahma turned to Lord Vishnu for assistance, and Vishnu took care of them. Then, Lord Vishnu told Brahma that the creation of negative energy is an inevitable byproduct of the creation of positive energy. As a result, Lord Vishnu advises Brahma to breed a superior race of people to serve as guardians for all humanity. There is an other account of the varnas' genesis in the Rig Veda. According to this Hindu text, the Brahmin race sprung from Brahma's mouth, whereas the Kshatriya race developed through the use of weapons.

Kshatriyas were responsible for ruling the country and fighting in battles, thus it seems sense that many members of this caste went into such fields. Kshatriya society placed a higher value on boys since they were seen as emblems of manhood, while girls were expected to be more submissive and respectful. Men and women of the other Varnas were not permitted to marry members of the Brahmin Varna. After the Brahmin, the Kshatriya caste is considered to be one of the most powerful in India. They watch to see that everyone remains in their Varna.

The End

9 798889 866794

Printed by Libri Plureos GmbH in Hamburg,
Germany